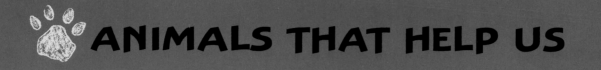

Animals Protecting Us

Robert Snedden

FRANKLIN WATTS
A Division of Grolier Publishing
NEW YORK • LONDON • HONG KONG • SYDNEY
DANBURY, CONNECTICUT

Picture Credits

Cover: Lancashire Constabulary

Interior Pictures: Corbis pp. 16 (Joseph Sohm; ChromoSohm Inc.), 17b (Hulton-Deutsch Collection), 21b (Vittoriano Rastelli), 28b (Bettmann/Reuters); Ecoscene p. 11b (Angela Hampton); Eye Ubiquitous pp. 5b (Gavin Wickham), 12b (Gary Trotter); Sally and Richard Greenhill p. 4; Robert Harding p. 13t (Shout); Hulton Getty Collection p. 5t; Impact Photos pp. 12t (Martin Black), 15t (Homer Sykes), 22 (Zak Waters), 23t (Brian Harris), 27b (Sally Fear); Only Horses p. 29b; Lancashire Constabulary pp. 10b, 20b, 20t, 20b, 21t, 24, 26, 27t, 29t; Metropolitan Police pp. 7t, 9t, 11t, 14t, 17t, 18, 19t, 19b, 28t; Rex Features pp. 6 (Today), 7b (Julian Makey), 8 (Greg Williams), 9b (Sipa/Sylvain Lefrevre), 10t, 13b (Sipa/Laif), 14b, 15b (Today), 23b (Sipa/Olivier Coret), 25t (Julian Makey), 25b (Sipa/Haley).

The Publishers would like to thank PC Philip Walsh of the Lancashire Constabulary Mounted Section and the photographic unit for setting up and taking the images showing the training of police horses

Series editor: Helen Lanz
Series designer: Louise Snowdon
Picture research: Sue Mennell

First published in 1999 by Franklin Watts
A Division of Grolier Publishing
90 Sherman Turnpike
Danbury, CT 06816

Visit Franklin Watts/Children's Press on the Internet at:
http://publishing.grolier.com

A catalog record for this title is available from the Library of Congress.

ISBN: 0-531-14561-1 (lib. bdg)   0-531-15406-8 (pbk)

Contents

Animal Officers

In police forces around the world, dogs and horses work together with human officers as part of a special team.

Dogs are naturally skilled at guarding, tracking, and hunting. These abilities are very useful in police work.

In the last hundred years, police forces all over the world have found out just how useful a trained police dog can be.

Dogs are naturally territorial — they like to protect their own space.

Police horses have been used in many countries since the 18th century.

Before cars were widely available, police forces used horses to patrol growing towns and cities.

An officer sitting 8 ft (2.5m) above the ground was in a good position to see what was happening all around him.

Dogs and horses also provide a good opportunity for the police and public to get to know and trust each other. People are interested in talking to an officer on horseback or to a dog handler. People always love to pet the animals.

Mounted police in Houston, Texas, chat with the public at a 4th of July celebration.

A Good Police Dog

Being a police dog is not easy. Out of every hundred dogs, perhaps only four or five will be accepted into the force.

Police dogs have to learn to behave well all the time, even when faced with tremendous temptation!

Dogs must be clever and eager to please. They need to be fit so they can chase and jump or climb over obstacles. Above all, police dogs must obey their handlers at all times.

German Shepherds are one of the most popular breeds for police dogs. They are strong, clever, and determined — just what is needed for the demands of police work.

Other dog breeds that work with the police include Labradors, Golden Retrievers, and Spaniels. These dogs are excellent at sniffing out dangerous materials such as bombs or drugs with their keen noses.

This Labrador is searching for drugs hidden in this car.

Dogs that are chosen to join the police force are not afraid of danger. They often risk being injured in order to protect their handlers, or when they help a member of the public.

Police dogs are trained to attack if told to do so by their handler.

Learning Together

Officers need at least two years' experience of police work before they can apply to become dog handlers. Then they have to be tested to make sure that they are suitable to work with dogs.

If successful, officers will be given a puppy to take home. The puppy will usually be about three months old.

> The puppy becomes part of the "puppy officer's" family.

The new handler is taught how to look after the puppy.

At about ten months to a year old, the dog will be tested to see if it will make a good police dog. Then it starts a training course.

Police dogs, like all dogs, start with the basics — walking to heel, sitting and staying, and lying down on command.

Of course, the dogs learn much more than this. By the end of three months of hard training, a police dog can follow a scent, chase and attack, control prisoners and crowds, and know what to do when faced with a weapon.

A large, well-trained dog is a great help in controlling a crowd.

Seeking and Finding

No matter how clean you are, a dog's sensitive nose can pick up your smell. To a dog, every person has his or her own particular scent. A dog can pick out the one person it is looking for from a crowd.

When a dog is tracking someone, it follows the scent that the person leaves behind in the air and on the ground.

A police dog learns how to follow a trail over many different types of ground, such as open country, farmland, woodland areas, city streets, and buildings. A dog can follow a scent in all types of weather.

Scent trails last longer in the countryside, where bushes and soft mud hold on to smells. In towns, scents quickly wear off hard surfaces such as pavement.

Tracking skills can be used to find criminals, missing people, or lost property.

When the dog finds the person or object it is looking for, it is trained to "give tongue" or "speak" — barking to bring its human partner to the spot.

Animal Anecdote

In 1996, in the state of Iowa, a police dog and some sheep teamed up to catch two men wanted for armed robbery.

One of the robbers had hidden in a haystack in a barn. When police officers went into the barn, the sheep were all looking right at the man's hiding place! The police dog tracked the second robber to his hiding place near a stream. The dog grabbed the robber, and he was successfully arrested.

Sniffing It Out

Most police forces have specially trained sniffer dogs.

Dogs love to play, so sniffer training starts off as a game. The trainer makes use of the dog's natural hunting instinct, or ability, and plays games such as hide-and-seek. Even searching for drugs and bombs seems like a game to the dog.

In training and in real work, the dog is rewarded when it finds what it is looking for.

Dogs can tell the difference between smells that to our noses seem the same. It is not known just how sensitive a dog's sense of smell is. It has been estimated that it is between 200 and 5 million times better than a human's sense of smell.

This dog is being trained to recognize the smell of different explosives.

A machine for detecting bombs at an airport costs about $100,000. A sniffer dog can be trained for less than $10,000.

A trained sniffer dog can pick out the one person in a crowd who is carrying drugs or explosives. And no machine can scamper over baggage on a moving conveyor belt the way a dog can!

Animal Anecdote

At one time, police in Germany used a trained pig to sniff out drugs and explosives!

Pigs are well known for their keen sense of smell. Luise, the sniffer pig, could find drugs hidden nearly 6½ feet (2 meters) underground.

You're Under Arrest!

Dog teams are often sent out to places where serious crimes have been reported, such as muggings, robberies, or riots.

All of these situations require police officers on the scene as quickly as possible.

On arrival, the dogs are usually very excited and are barking and growling.

Police dogs are used to chase and grab people who are trying to escape.

An angry dog is often enough to frighten those who are causing the trouble. But if necessary, police dogs are trained to bring down someone who tries to escape or fight.

Sometimes the people causing problems are gone by the time the police arrive. Then the officer in charge will decide whether it is necessary to release the dog to do a search.

Dog and handler work together — the handler guides the dog to make sure it doesn't go back over ground it has already covered.

A dog can search a large building or area much more quickly than its human partner.

Animal Anecdote

British police dog Khan never gave up the chase. Once when running after two men, he was hit by a car and trapped underneath it. As soon as he was freed, he was off again.

Despite an injured leg, he managed to catch the men he was after.

A Good Police Horse

Many police forces around the world have a mounted section — a department of police officers who patrol on horseback.

Each force obtains its horses in different ways. Some horses are donated, or given, by members of the public. Forces like the famous Royal Canadian Mounted Police (the Mounties) have their own breeding stables.

It isn't easy to be accepted as a police horse. Out of the 600 horses offered each year to the Los Angeles Police Department, in the State of California, only about six are accepted.

A horse that is accepted for police training will usually be between 3 and 5 years old, and over 15 hands high (one hand is about 4 in, or 10 cm).

A good horse will be lively but calm. It must get used to working in often noisy and sometimes dangerous situations.

Animal Anecdote

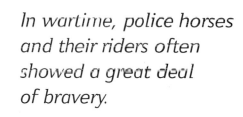

In wartime, police horses and their riders often showed a great deal of bravery.

During the Second World War (1939-1945), a horse called Upstart stayed calm even though he was startled by a shower of glass and metal from a bomb explosion just 230 feet (70 meters) away.

Horse and Rider

Officers have to be in the police force for at least two years before they can join the mounted section. There is often a lot of competition to be a mounted police officer. In some forces only one officer in five who apply for mounted duty will be accepted.

It is not necessary for the trainee mounted police officers to know a lot about horses. Once they have been accepted, the officers go through a tough training course. They will change horses several times to get used to riding different mounts.

As part of training, horse and rider experience what it might be like to be in a riot.

Training cannot cover everything that might happen on police duty. The most important thing is that the horse should trust its rider and do as it is told.

After five months of hard work, the new mounted police officers are ready to take their horses out on patrol for the first time.

The mounted section of a police force is usually quite small. The Metropolitan Police in London have about 150 horses and officers. This is more than half the police horses in all of Britain.

Most mounted sections are based in big cities.

Going to School

Training a new police horse can take several months. Each horse is different, and each one is given its own training program. This allows the horse to learn at its own pace.

Horses are taught to allow their riders to open gates on horseback.

A police horse must keep calm in crowds and not be frightened by sudden noises, movement, or lights.

Trainers make loud noises, let off fireworks, flash lights, wave flags, and do all the things that a horse will experience on duty.

The horse is made to walk over different surfaces so that it won't refuse to walk somewhere when on patrol.

Gradually, each horse becomes more confident and will accept different and strange sights and sounds.

All through its training, the horse will be encouraged and rewarded.

When a horse is ready to go out in public, an experienced police rider will take it out onto the streets of the town or city where it will work. Here the horse completes its final training on the job.

An experienced horse will usually go with the trainee horse to give it confidence.

In countries where the police are armed, a horse must get used to a gun being fired from its back.

21

Crowd Control

Police horses and riders often have to deal with huge crowds of people.

Sometimes the crowd will be friendly — for example, at a street party or outdoor show.

At other times the police may face rioters, who might be throwing stones, bottles, and other weapons.

One advantage of being on horseback is that it allows the mounted police officer to spot troublemakers more easily.

The police use the horses' large size to control groups of people. Horse and rider are trained to walk sideways into a crowd — this makes people move without causing anyone any harm.

A mounted officer is worth twelve officers on the ground when it comes to crowd control.

Rioters often run off when they see police horses coming toward them.

Police dogs in France keep this soccer fan in order.

Dogs also play a part in crowd control. They are usually restrained, or held back, by their handlers, but they are allowed to jump up, bark, and growl at any troublemakers. If someone runs off, the dogs will be released to chase them.

23

In the Line of Duty

No police officer puts his or her animal partner in danger if it can be avoided. However, there are more dangers and risks to be faced in police work than there are in most ordinary jobs. Police horses and dogs face these dangers just as often as the human officers.

On crowd control duty, horses wear clear, tough plastic face guards to protect their eyes, in the same way human officers do.

Police animals can be injured while they are doing their job, no matter how much care is taken. Dog handlers and mounted officers are trained to give first aid to their partners.

Members of the public sometimes become quite attached to a police horse they see regularly. Get-well cards and flowers have been sent to a police stable when a horse has been injured.

Bomb sniffer dogs are given coats for protection just in case a bomb goes off unexpectedly.

All dog-handling and mounted sections have vets who can be called upon if necessary. An injured police animal will be given the best possible care and attention.

Off-Duty Care

A normal patrol for horse and rider might last around three hours.

Mounted police officers' duties do not end when they return to the stables, however.

Each horse is brushed, or groomed, whether it goes out on duty or not.

Back at the yard, the police horses need to be groomed and fed. The tack — the bridles and saddles — is cleaned. Learning about the proper care of a horse and how to look after its equipment is all part of the training for a mounted police officer. All the officers help keep the stables clean.

The horses are very well cared for. Each police force has its own farrier, a person who fixes horses' shoes. He or she makes sure that the horses' feet are in good condition.

In the winter, the horses are clipped (their coats are shaved) so if they get hot and sweat as they work, they can be kept clean more easily.

A police dog and its handler usually live together in the handler's home — so being a dog handler is a seven-day-a-week job. Even when not on duty, the police officer must make sure that the dog is given at least an hour's exercise every day. The officer must also make sure the dog has a healthy, balanced diet.

The Job Done

A dog is retired from police service when it is between 8 and 10 years old. It will stay with its human partner, living in the home as a family pet.

A sniffer or a tracker dog will often be able to work longer than a more active patrol dog.

If a dog's handler leaves the dog patrol section of the police force, the dog is usually retired. It is very difficult for someone to work with another officer's dog because of the strong friendship that forms between a dog and its handler.

Many police horses never actually retire, but as they get older the amount of time they spend on patrol will get shorter. Often older horses are kept in reserve at the stables. They will be exercised regularly, and sometimes they might be needed to help the younger horses with crowd control.

Some police forces sell their retired horses. Although they might not be fit enough for police work, they still make good riding horses.

Other mounted sections prefer to let their horses live out the rest of their lives in a familiar place, surrounded by the people that they have served well during their lives.

Glossary

criminals	people who have broken the law by doing something such as stealing.
determined	strong-willed; concentrating on what you are doing so you achieve what it is you want to do.
grooming	the action of looking after something, making it look neat and clean.
hand	the unit of length to measure the height of a horse; a hand is 4 in (10 cm).
handler	the police officer who is in charge of, or who handles, a police dog.
mugging	an attack on a person, usually to rob them.
patrol	moving around an area to make sure everything is as it should be.
reserve	something that is held for possible use later.
retired	having left a job at the end of your working life.
scent	a smell or odor.
tracking	following a trail left by someone.
trainee	someone who is training, or learning to do something.

Useful addresses

Dogs Against Drugs/Dogs Against Crime National Law Enforcement K-9 Association

http://www.daddac.com/
517 Spring Mills Road
Anderson, IN 46013

Provides funding for special purpose dogs and related equipment to police agencies throughout the United States and Canada.

K-9 World of Dogs

wysiwyg://34/http://www.w-dog.com/
5343 Stull Road
Petersburg, MI 49270
Offers an extensive dog training facility for police K-9 units, plus supplies and education.

National Police Bloodhound Association

http://www.icubed.com/~npba/
A non-profit organization dedicated to the advancement of the bloodhound in the field of law enforcement and search and rescue.

United States Police Canine Association

http://www.minn.net/uspca
8480 Cooper Way East
Inver Grove Heights,
MN 55076

Standardizes training methods to improve the abilities of dogs in police work.

Index